CHINESE STORIES
FOUR MAJOR CONTRIBUTIONS

Paper

Edited by Li Chaodong

Illustrated by Zou Jiahui

Translated by Xuemeng Angela Li

Books Beyond Boundaries

ROYAL COLLINS

Initially, ancient people used materials readily available to them, such as leaves and rocks.

Pottery pigsty of Han Dynasty (206 BC–AD 220)—the hut next to the pigsty is the toilet.

Later, standalone toilets were built, and people started using whittled bamboo and wooden pieces as cleansing tools. These materials were uncomfortable, leading to the gradual adoption of paper as a preferred cleaning material.

Yet, paper wasn't originally invented for this purpose.

What did our ancestors write on before paper was invented?

During the Shang Dynasty (1600–1046 BC), characters were carved on oracle bones to record divinations, marking the origin of the oracle bone script. Later on, bronze wares were used for inscriptions, though their solid texture made them hard to carve.

Later, people wrote on bamboo slips. However, bamboo slips were cumbersome, prone to dampness and insect damage, and difficult to carry, store, and organize.

Fine silk was another medium, but its high cost rendered it unaffordable for most people.

During the Western Han Dynasty (206 BC–AD 25), the paper was invented, solving many of these problems.

Initially, the earliest paper, made from discarded hemp, was coarse and unsuitable for writing. It was primarily used for wrapping items such as spices and traditional Chinese medicine.

Cai Lun unlocked the potential of paper for writing.

In the Eastern Han Dynasty (AD 25–220), Cai Lun improved papermaking processes after traveling and gathering knowledge across the country.

Using materials like tree bark, hemp remnants, worn-out cloth, and fishing nets, he reduced papermaking costs and made paper more accessible.

Later, Cai Lun was granted the title of "Marquis of Longting," and his paper became known as "Marquis Cai's Paper."

The use of paper made information transmission much more convenient. In the past, messages were passed by word of mouth, which often led to errors. Another method was using beacon fires, as seen in the story of "Beacon Fires Tricking the Lords."

After the invention of paper, people began writing letters instead. The use of carrier pigeons not only ensured speed and accuracy but also safeguarded privacy.

("Three" [*san*] has a similar pronunciation to "mountain" [*shan*] in Chinese, which sometimes causes confusion during oral exchange.)

The imperial court used to rely on bamboo slips for recording laws and official documents, which were heavy and took a long time to transport. Since paper was invented for writing, the court introduced official reports to deliver military updates and political orders quickly. This format has been considered the earliest newspaper format in China. The emperor then completed most of the communications with officials through paper documentation.

The widespread adoption of paper allowed people to express ideas and emotions in writing, fostering the creation and circulation of essays and rhapsodies.

During the Western Jin Dynasty (AD 265–317), poet Zuo Si's "Rhapsody on Three Capitals" became so popular that paper sold out across Luoyang, giving rise to the idiom "Paper Becomes Expensive in Luoyang."

The paper also promoted the development of Buddhism in China. Previously, the spread of Buddhism relied mainly on the recitation of scriptures. From the Wei and Jin dynasties (AD 220–420) to the early Tang Dynasty (AD 618–907), Chinese monks initiated a fervent movement to journey west in search of Buddhist teachings. They utilized lightweight paper to copy a large number of Buddhist scriptures, ensuring their preservation and dissemination.

Literature works were more widely disseminated thanks to paper, and literati could carry lightweight paper to record their creations. For example, during the Northern Wei Dynasty (AD 386–534), geographer Li Daoyuan was able to write as he traveled, producing the monumental work *Commentary on the Waterways Classic*.

Writing on bamboo slips constrained character size and required precision due to limited space.

The invention of paper, with its excellent ink absorption and larger surface, enabled the development of diverse calligraphy styles, such as regular script and cursive script.

The rise of calligraphy masters like Wang Xizhi and Wang Xianzhi during the Eastern Jin Dynasty (AD 317–420) was largely attributed to the widespread use of paper.

During the Sui (AD 581–618) and Tang dynasties, the high demand for Buddhist scriptures led to the invention of woodblock printing, reducing book production costs and promoting cultural development.

Woodblock printing

With improved access to books, education became more widespread, enabling more people to qualify as government officials through the Imperial Examination. Practices like presenting name cards also gained popularity.

Write on the sand with reeds to teach one's son

Announcement of successful examinees of the Imperial Examination

The widespread use and refinement of paper also influenced the development of painting.

Decorative paper

During the Qin (221–206 BC) and Han dynasties, paintings were typically done on silk to avoid penetration of the ink into the fabric, and painters often used fine line drawing or double-outline techniques to fill in the colors. A very limited amount of painters had access to silk drawing due to its high cost at the time.

After the Sui and Tang dynasties, people improved papermaking technology and invented rice paper known for its excellent ink absorption and the ability to create watercolor-like effects. It allowed artists to freely express themselves, giving rise to the distinct style of a landscape-free sketch.

Refined scholars also produced and adopted their own specially processed decorative paper for writing and painting.

The promotion of paper also advanced technology development.

On the one hand, paper-based books such as *Tiangong Kaiwu* and *Qimin Yaoshu* compiled ancient technological knowledge, laying the foundation for many great inventions and innovations in later generations.

On the other hand, papermaking became a profitable industry with some towns emerging due to papermaking. Later, book printing and binding industries also appeared, providing the common people with new means of livelihood and marking the early beginnings of the paper industry.

The increased variety and production of paper enabled it to fulfill people's needs beyond cultural and social life, becoming integrated into all aspects of their daily lives.

The appearance of toilet paper created a more hygienic cleaning experience for using the toilet.

Ancient people also started to wrap paper around items such as mirrors and porcelain, which were prone to scratching or breaking.

Nowadays, we still wrap shoes in this way.

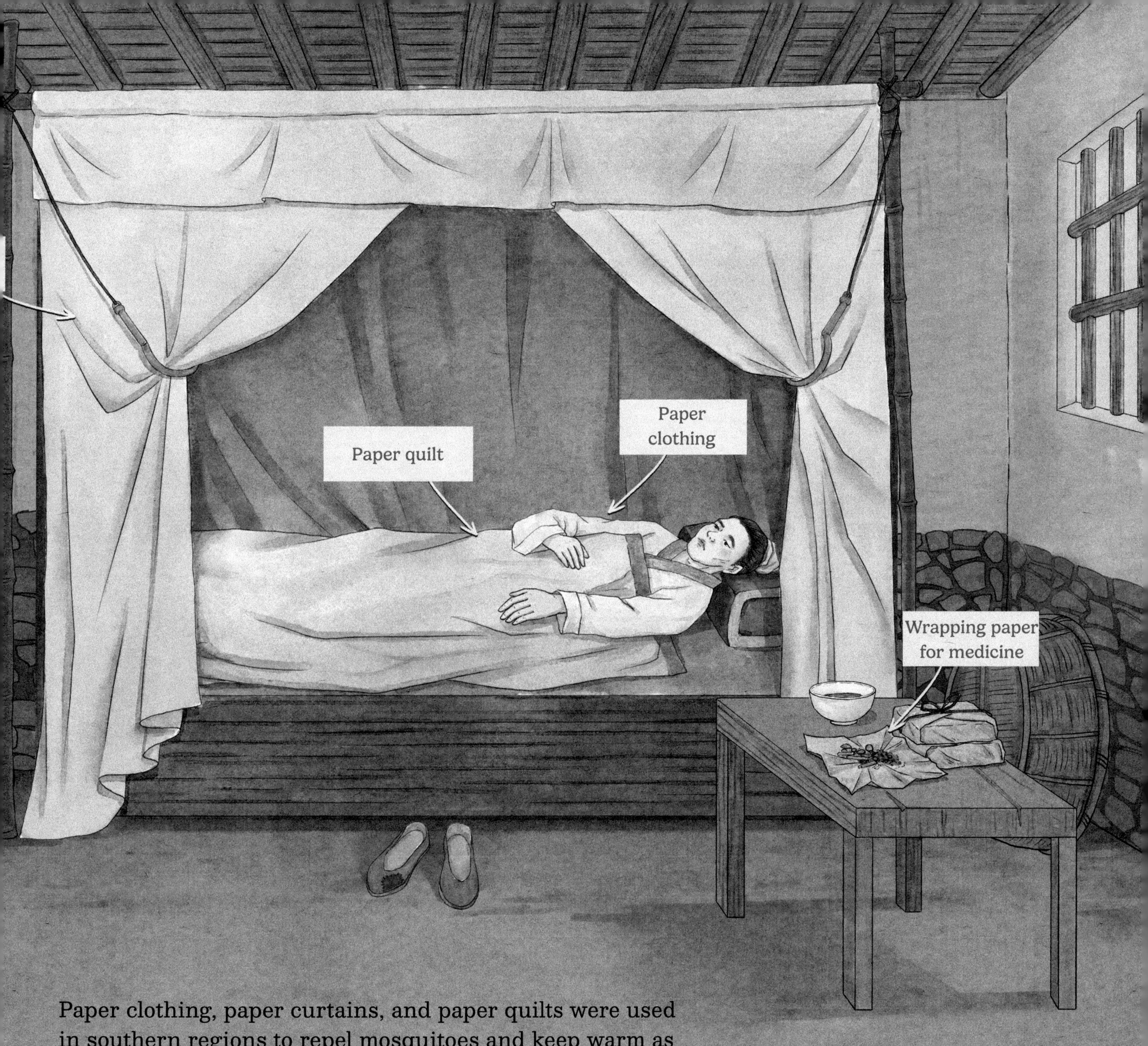

Paper clothing, paper curtains, and paper quilts were used in southern regions to repel mosquitoes and keep warm as substitutes for the more expensive silk products.

Oil-paper umbrellas, lanterns, and window paper demonstrated excellent waterproof and light-transmitting properties.

Paper could also be used to make various toys, such as kites, shadow puppets, and leaf cards, which the ancient Chinese people loved.

Paper fans were companions of refined scholars where they would inscribe poems, calligraphy, and paintings. The exquisite craftsmanship of paper fans, combined with traditional calligraphy, poetry, and artwork, made them objects of great admiration and fondness.

During the Song Dynasty (AD 960–1279), rapid economic development led to significant improvements in papermaking and printing quality. This era saw the emergence of the earliest Chinese paper currency—*jiaozi*. Paper money began to replace cumbersome copper coins, paving the way for expanded commercial trade and facilitating currency circulation on a global scale in later generations.

After the paper spread to other countries, it has gone through significant development.

As early as the Wei, Jin, and Northern and Southern Dynasties (AD 420–581) period, papermaking techniques were introduced to the Korean Peninsula. The ancient Koreans produced Korean Paper, which not only met their domestic needs but was also sent back to China as a tribute and was highly valued and welcomed by the Chinese.

Korean paper

In the 6th and 7th centuries, Chinese treatises on papermaking began to be introduced to Japan. The exchange of paper between China and Japan facilitated the communication of scientific and cultural knowledge and fostered friendly relations between the two countries.

It is said that in AD 751, a battle occurred near the city of Talas (in present-day Kazakhstan) between the Tang Dynasty and the Arab Caliphate (known as Dashi in Chinese). After the battle, some Tang soldiers were captured, among whom some were skilled papermakers. The Arabs thus learned papermaking techniques through these captives.

However, as a cultural and technological innovation, the spread of papermaking could not have been achieved through a single battle. In fact, as early as the Han Dynasty, when the Silk Road was first built, paper had already begun to spread westward through commercial exchanges along the road.

After the Arabs learned about papermaking, the paper quickly spread throughout the Arab region, gradually replacing the previously used papyrus.

Using paper, the Arabs translated many books from both Eastern and Western cultures. At that time, the Arab region had the highest number of libraries worldwide. Concepts like algebra and the decimal system emerged during this period too.

The paper made by the Arabs not only supplied local demand but was also exported to Europe and the Eastern Roman Empire, becoming an important trade item for Samarkand. In Cairo, Egypt, paper—this new invention—could be seen everywhere at that time.

It looks like the Europeans took several hundreds of years to fully adopt paper.

Previously, European countries primarily used Egyptian papyrus or parchment for writing. Parchment was an expensive writing material; for example, copying a Bible required approximately 300 sheets of parchment. The high cost of writing materials severely limited the spread of culture and information, hindering the development of European civilization.

Because of that, during the Middle Ages, the Europeans remained ignorant for a long time and endured oppression.

When papermaking technology was introduced, Europe began to undergo dramatic changes. So, how was papermaking introduced to Europe?

This started with a paper mill in Damascus established by the Arab Empire. Due to its proximity to the Mediterranean and convenient transportation network, European countries all began purchasing paper from Damascus.

However, Europeans were reluctant to spend large amounts of metal currency to buy paper from the Arabs every year. Thus they planned to establish their own papermaking industry.

Spain was the first European country to make paper, but it was the Arabs who initially established many paper mills there. Later, when the Spanish reconquered their territories, Europeans took over the papermaking tradition from the Arabs. In Italy, papermaking technology was directly introduced from Egypt, and the establishment of the paper industry significantly boosted Italy's cultural development. By the 14th century, Italy had become a major paper supplier in Europe.

With the advent of papermaking, Europeans gained access to affordable books, leading to the establishment of a significant number of universities and providing more people with opportunities for education.

On the one hand, people began exploring nature and translating works, driving the continuous development of natural sciences. The cultural and scientific literacy of the Europeans also steadily improved, laying a solid foundation for the coming Industrial Revolution.

On the other hand, as the minds of the Europeans were liberated, dissatisfaction with royal and religious rule grew, leading Europe into a period of political revolutions.

In the late 16th century, the Spanish established paper mills in Mexico, introducing papermaking technology to the Americas.

After German inventor Gutenberg improved printing technology, the revolutionary significance of paper was further amplified. As a medium for spreading civilization, paper profoundly influenced the development of global civilization.

Paper is the long-term accumulation and crystallization of life experience and wisdom from the ancient Chinese working people. Its invention and application played an extremely important role in the exchange and dissemination of culture and ideologies, as well as the progress and development of human civilization.

In modern society, paper still plays an important role. Writing requires paper, hand hygiene depends on tissue paper, and sending parcels involves using cardboard boxes. A wide variety of paper products enrich our lives with diversity.

Chinese Stories: Four Major Contributions

Paper

Edited by Li Chaodong
Illustrated by Zou Jiahui
Translated by Xuemeng Angela Li

First published in 2024 by Royal Collins Publishing Group Inc.
Groupe Publication Royal Collins Inc.
550-555 boul. René-Lévesque O Montréal (Québec) H2Z1B1 Canada

10 9 8 7 6 5 4 3 2 1

ISBN: 978-1-4878-1328-4

To find out more about our publications, please visit www.royalcollins.com.

About the Editor

LI CHAODONG, born in 1963, is a prominent figure in China's education publishing industry and a graduate of the Department of History at East China Normal University. Over his distinguished career, he has edited and published more than 50 book series. He has been honored as a "National Leading Talent in Press and Publication" and recognized as "China's Annual Publication Figure." Li currently serves as the Founding Vice President of the All-China Federation of Industry and Commerce Book Industry Chamber of Commerce, Vice President of the Fifth Council of the China Book Publishing Association, and Vice Chairman of both the Anhui and Jiangsu Publishing Associations.